The Meaning of Life

A Child's Book of Existential Psychology

JULIAN LEV

With Images by Zara Kriegstein

TRANS LIMBIC PRESS

The Meaning of Life
A Child's Book of Existential Psychology

For information write Trans Limbic Press
PO Box 760, Tijeras, New Mexico 87059.
www.xpsychforkids.com

ISBN: 978-0-9794108-1-9
Library of Congress Control Number: 2007901725

For those who would like to apply these principles to solve
personal problems, the author recommends that you first
consult a mental health professional.

When we are born, we are not issued a manual on what it means to be human. We have no explanation for our existence or for our purpose here. Nevertheless, no matter who we are—whatever sex, race, nationality, or religion—no matter our age or even our intelligence, as long as we have the capacity to think, we find ourselves filled with questions about who we are, why we are, or whether we should be at all. Our very existence seems to demand that we define a place for ourselves here. It is our approach to this problem of our existence that defines who we are as individuals. This collaboration of literature and art is an exploration of the psychology of existence in basic terms, as a child might present it, if he or she had the pictures and words available.

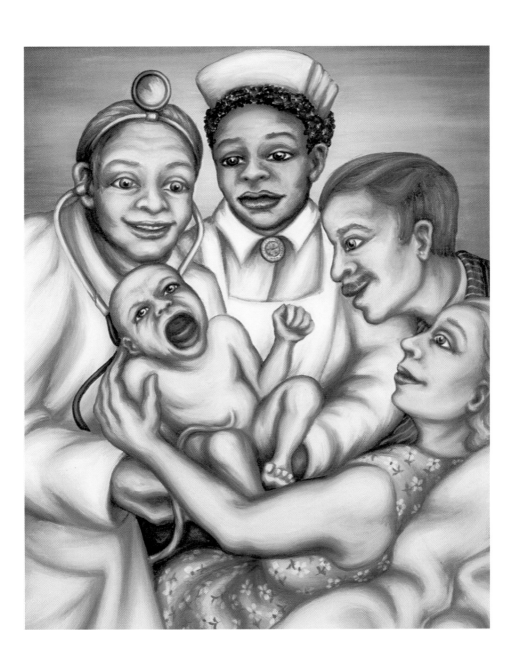

In the beginning everyone is born.

The doctor is born. The nurse is born.
The policeman is born.

The garbageman is born. Daddy is born.
Even mommy is born.

And you're born, too.

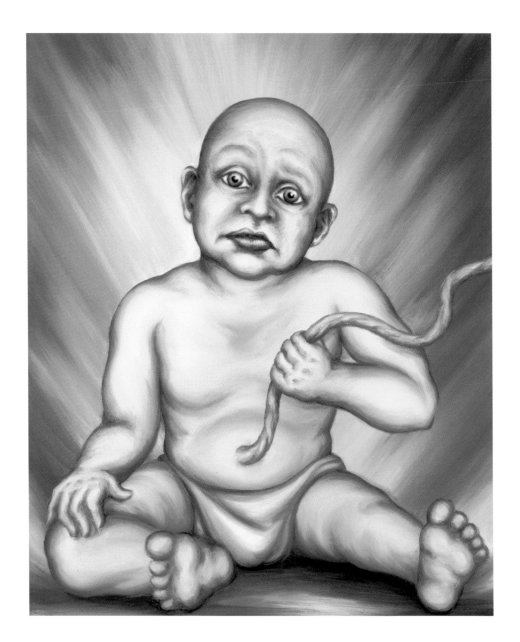

Some people know what they want to be when they are very small.

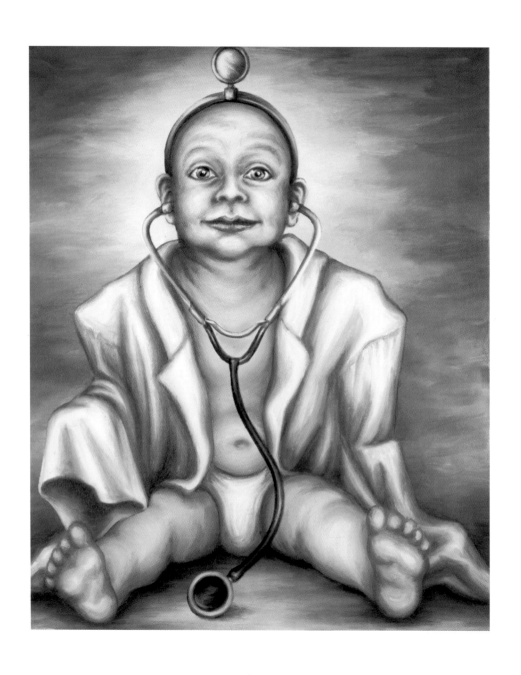

I want to be a doctor!

They decide what they want to be.

Then they go out and do it.

What do you want to be?

I don't know!

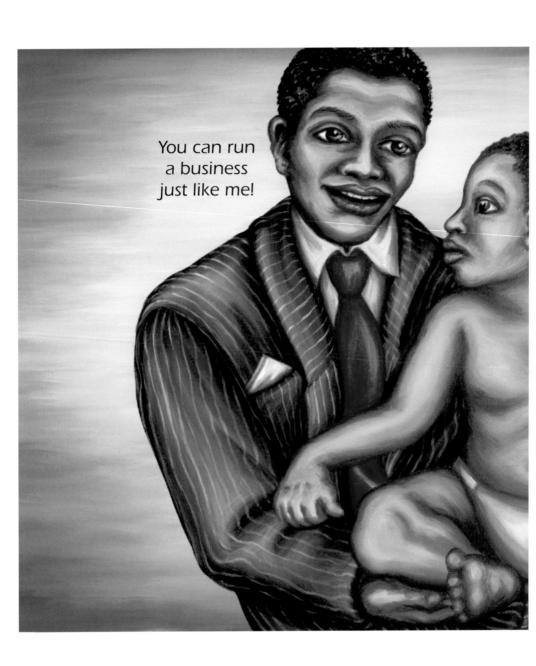

You could be what Mommy and Daddy
want you to be.

But being like Mommy or Daddy
just won't do. It's boring.
They never get to have any fun.
Besides, you just don't like
wearing a suit...

For a while it seems
that some questions have no answers
and it can be that way for a
very, Very, VERY long time...

I don't want to be anybody!

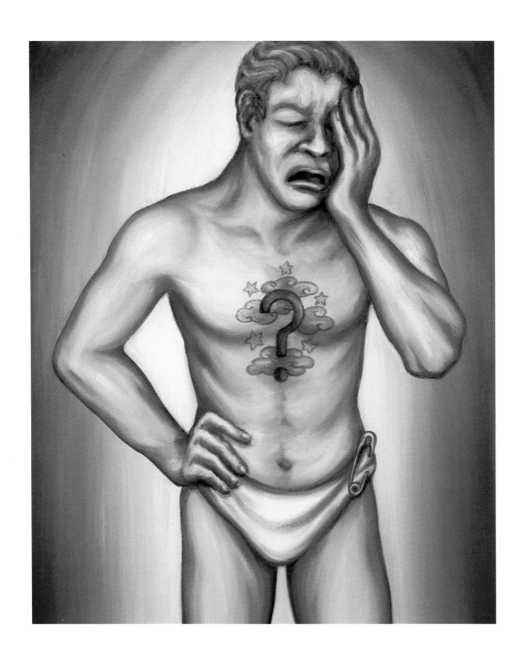

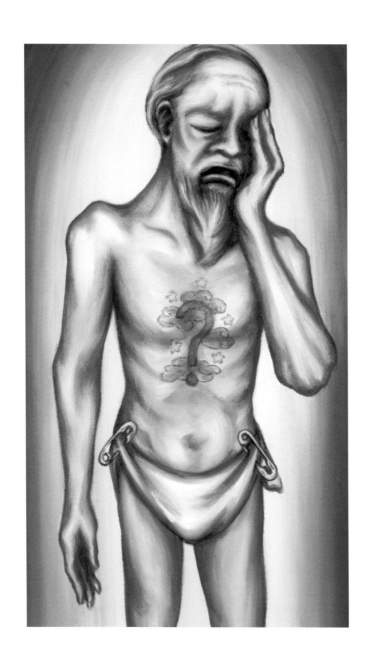

But then, you can't find an answer
if you go around crying all the time.
You have to stop sometime!!!

And if you're quiet, if you're *very* quiet,
you can open your eyes and an answer will
be there...or the start or the end of one.

And if you follow the cord...

The *very* long cord...

You'll end up at the beginning again.

And we each have our own Mom and Dad...
and they have their moms and dads.

It runs in the family.

I wanted to be a gangster.
Now, I'm a computer programmer.

I wanted to be a ballerina.
Now, I'm the head of a big business.

And if you try hard,
you'll go back before the beginning
along many cords...

Until you find the answer.

I don't know what I want
to be. Can you tell me?

I don't know what
I want to be either.

I followed my cord...   So did I.

You created every-
thing and you still
don't know what
you want to be?

I made everything you see
except for this cord. Maybe when
I come to the end of the cord, I'll
find out what I should be…

Sometimes the simplest questions are the hardest to answer. But, don't give up! You never know when you might find a clue. Your search can lead you anywhere. So, keep your eyes open! Put on your detective hat and pay very careful attention. It is a very, Very, VERY long cord...

Julian Lev is a licensed psychologist who practices in Albuquerque, New Mexico. He received his doctorate in Counseling Psychology from Ball State University in Muncie, Indiana in 1989. Dr. Lev's practice is based on his conviction that, for all our individual differences, we share many common experiences and problems. If placed in proper context, these experiences will reveal deeper meanings that can be understood by almost anyone.

Zara Kriegstein received her Master of Fine Arts degree in painting from the Academy of Art in West Berlin in 1978. She spent a year traveling through Italy, Turkey, Iraq, Pakistan, India, Nepal, Malaysia, and Mexico to study the art and culture of ancient civilizations. Her style of painting combines German Expressionism and Mexican mural painting. She lives and paints in Santa Fe, New Mexico.